Autumn Blues

Fatimah Ibn-Ali

Presentation by *BookLeaf Publishing*

Web: www.bookleafpub.com

E-mail: info@bookleafpub.com

ISBN: 9789357212069

First edition 2023

ACKNOWLEDGEMENT

I would like to thank my sisters, Kay and Junie, for never giving up on me and for always being my cheerleaders when it came to my poetry.

Broken Heart

I gently cradle
broken pieces of my heart
in my shaking hands.
I feel warm wetness
seeping out between my fingers.
I think it must be the blood
draining from my heart,
but it's just the tears
of my weeping soul,
filling my eyes,
running down my face,
salty and bitter.

Trapped Words

There are poems in me
trying to reach the surface,
words trying to express my pain.
My loneliness looks for companions
among the letters of the alphabet.
In the dying sunlight,
a cold autumn breeze rattles my bones.
My pen is dry,
my pages blank,
I don't have the strength
to write anymore.
I feel so invisible,
a ghost in the dusky gloom.
I wonder if this is how I'll always be,
a writer imprisoned in her mind's tomb.

Tears

Silent tears gather
at the edge of my lashes,
two shimmering pools
in the dim light of the moon,
they leave ghostly traces
upon my cheeks.
No one could tell
no matter how closely they looked,
but I can feel the path they took,
dried out by the wind.
Broken hearts
hide in plain sight,
in broad daylight,
but most people can't see.

Without You

Life without you is dull.
It's a gloomy rainstorm,
dark grey clouds,
weeping windows,
and cold clammy darkness.
Hope fades
as I wait for sunshine.
It never breaks through
the heavy blanket of fog.
I'm left stranded in the storm,
alone and chilled to the bone.

Fragments

Broken hearts,
scattered dreams,
splintered memories,
shattered souls.
Lives are made up of pieces,
glued together by frantic,
trembling fingers
and bandaged hands.
People seek peace and solace,
in the fragments of their fragile existences.

Dark Hope

Everyone talks about hope
like it's the miracle of life.
But no one talks about
the dark side of hope,
the hope that fights so intensely,
the hope that crushes your ribs
and chokes the breath out of you,
the hope that sits like a rock
in the pit of your stomach
and claws at your throat,
the hope that tries to cling on,
even though there is none left,
the hope that nearly kills you.

Graveyard

My heart is a graveyard
full of buried hopes,
the grounds haunted
by ghosts of loves unrequited.
Broken dreams,
like shattered glass,
lie scattered among the tombstones.
Rivers of pain,
weep through the cracks of loneliness,
the wind sighs and whispers
tales of woes,
throughout the barren hills of disappointment.

Giving Up

I feel myself giving up.
My heart aches,
but I've stopped fighting.
My racing thoughts are quieter,
my sadness silent.
My soul weeps,
and a tear slowly trickles down my cheek,
but I've given up.
Hope sits with her head bent,
shoulders slumped,
face hidden in her tired hands.
There's just no point.
If only love was enough.
If only everyone got lucky.

Gone Away

If I am gone
by the time you come back,
cry not for I have been faithful.
I waited as long as you told me to,
and then I waited some more.
I believed in you,
but you forgot me
and were nowhere to be found.
So life came and took me,
and away I have gone.

The Sea

I've always loved the sea.
When I looked into your eyes,
I saw oceans alive,
staring back at me.
It was wonderful
to see something I loved,
reflected in you.
And I loved you,
but you weren't meant to be mine.
Now when I look out to sea,
I see your beautiful eyes,
and I am burdened with sadness.
You are reflected in the waters
I once loved so much,
but now you and the sea are one,
ruthless reminders of my pain.

Helpless

Sometimes,
I clearly see
my world falling apart.
And there's nothing,
absolutely nothing,
that I can do to stop it.
Sometimes,
I hardly know who I am,
where I'm supposed to go,
or who I'm meant to be.
It leaves me feeling
lost, scared, and empty.

Survivor

She smiles wistfully
as she blinks back tears.
She's not unfamiliar
with saying goodbye to things she loves.
She's experienced heartbreak before,
and she's survived.
She will survive again.
She will get through the pain.
She will silently wrestle
with the actual depth of despair,
in which sinks
her bruised and aching heart.

Love's Ghost

I hear his voice
calling out goodbyes,
we wanted to get home,
somewhere warm and dry,
away from the blustery snow of winter.

I feel his breath
warming my cold fingers,
we thought the rain couldn't hurt us,
after all we were young,
and spring was in the air.

I hear his laugh
ringing through the empty streets,
we used to walk these roads,
hand in hand,
in love with the warmth of summer.

I feel his whisper
brushing across my cheek,
we stood still,
silent and enraptured,
by the red harvest moon of autumn.

Four seasons, that's how long I knew him.
Now I'm left with his ghost,
haunting memories of his beautiful eyes,
his fragrance lingering in my clothes,
and a longing for something that never was.

Bleeding Hands

Everyone came to her with their troubles.
She wrapped her arms around them,
wiped away countless tears,
let their sadness seep into her shoulders.
She patched up their bleeding wounds,
helped pick up pieces of their broken hearts,
gently removed their sharp shards of misery.
She never looked at her own hands,
covered in bright red gashes,
she never noticed her own shoulders,
slumped with grief and agony,
she never realized her own heart,
frayed and tired and alone.

Shipwreck

I stand on the shoreline,
my heart breaking every night.
The waves crash noisily,
telling the story of your plight.
The rocks glisten with sea spray,
like your dear eyes in moonlight.
The wind whips up a frenzy,
the rain soaks me to the bone.
The tears stream down my face,
I know, I'm all alone.

It's All Lies

I sit on the bathroom floor,
tears streaming down my face,
hugging my knees to my chest.
I stand up straight and tall,
wash the pain away,
and go out to meet the world.
I keep moving forward,
one step at a time,
telling myself it's going to be okay,
saying that at the end,
it will be worth all the pain.
That's what they always say,
when building warriors and survivors.
But what if the pain doesn't go away?
What if the tears are for nothing?
What if my heart breaks
and keeps breaking until it's all dust?
What if life is just pain,
and we're lying to ourselves,
simply to survive?

Tired

When I crash onto the rocks,
as I do every now and then,
I want to lie there,
wounded and crushed.
I want to bleed out,
as I watch the sunset,
bright and radiant.
I want to hear the soft
whoosh of the waves,
as the view becomes hazy
and my eyes close,
perhaps forever.
I don't want to be strong,
resilient, or brave.

No Heroes

You cannot save people,
not the ones you love,
not the ones you don't love.
You just can't.
It's not up to you.
They're going to live their fate.
They'll make their mistakes.
They'll slip, and fall,
and get hurt.
You cannot stop one bit of it.
You can only be there,
to listen when they speak,
to hold their hearts safe
and their hands tight,
if, and when, they choose you.

Forever Hurting

They say time heals all wounds.
It's not entirely true.
After a while,
it just becomes socially improper
to keep grieving.
So people collect
the jagged pieces of their pain,
and bury it all away
deep in their chests.
The sharp stab eventually goes away,
but there remains a dull ache,
forever reminding you of your hurt
with every throbbing heartbeat.

Submission

There are a couple of things
you can always be sure of:
disappointment, loss, and death.
The world has asked me,
time and again,
to stop fighting fate and give in,
give in to giving up people, places, and things.
I struggle every time,
hoping that my desperation
will convince the universe
to hear me out, to have mercy.
So far, I've lost all the battles.
I end up too tired to argue,
I prepare myself to brave the changes.
With quiet tears and a broken heart,
I yield.
I concede.
I submit.

Last Goodbye

She smiles at him, softly,
her eyes tracing the curves
of his laughing mouth,
the sweep of his long lashes.
"Peace out," he says,
ready to fly,
ready to dive,
into all that life has to offer.
"Just be safe," she says,
her tone level,
her voice slightly bored,
attempting to mask
the flurry of emotions
rushing through her veins,
as she watches him disappear
into the horizon,
for the last time.
Three little words,
replacing the three she really wants to say,
but she can't.
The words are locked in her throat,
and only he holds the key.